HOW TO

CIRCUMVENT A SECURITY ALARM

in 10 SECONDS or Less

An Insider's Guide to How It's Done and How to Prevent It

B. ANDY

PALADIN PRESS
BOULDER, COLORADO

How to Circumvent a Security Alarm in 10 Seconds or Less:
An Insider's Guide to How It's Done and How to Prevent It
by B. Andy

Copyright © 1994 by B. Andy

ISBN 0-87364-777-7
Printed in the United States of America

Published by Paladin Press, a division of
Paladin Enterprises, Inc., P.O. Box 1307,
Boulder, Colorado 80306, USA.
(303) 443-7250

Direct inquiries and/or orders to the above address.

Contents

Disclaimer

SOME OF THE TECHNIQUES DESCRIBED IN THIS BOOK ARE illegal. They are also dangerous. Whenever dealing with electricity or electric devices, special precautions *must* be followed in accordance with industry standards for service and experimentation. Failure to strictly follow such industry standards may result in harm to life or limb.

Therefore, the author, publisher, and distributors of this book disclaim any liability for any damages or injuries of any type that a reader or user of information contained within this book may encounter from the use of said information. It is presented for academic study and information purposes only!

Introduction

YOU MIGHT ASK WHY SOMEONE WOULD WRITE A BOOK THAT could demonstrate how to circumvent an alarm system in 10 seconds or less. The intention really isn't to teach you how to get around or through a security system. It isn't even designed to serve as a technical manual. The true purpose is to teach you how to make your security system more secure. I think the best way to learn how to make an alarm system more secure is to learn how to compromise its weak areas.

If you don't currently own an alarm system, this book will show you step by step what to look for when purchasing one. By reading this book and following the simple circumvention techniques, you will know what to look for in designing your own security system, whether it be for your home or business.

Unfortunately, designing the right system for your particular life-style is not quite as simple as it sounds. Why? In some cases, the alarm salesperson isn't knowledgeable enough to assist you in determining the correct design. Sad to say, but true. Most care about earning a commission, not securing your home in the best possible way. In all fairness, there are a few who do try; however, most alarm salespeople go through no formalized training to learn about what they sell and cannot be classified as security professionals.

The little training that is offered to salespeople in the alarm industry has more to do with generating sales leads, closing sales, and getting you to sign a contract. I write from experience, as I have worked in all facets of the security industry for the past 14 years. Not to blow my own horn, but my background encompasses both technical and ownership experience.

Some may think that I have an ax to grind with the industry. Not so. This industry has been very good to me and my family. Unfortunately, it's a highly segmented industry. Last count, there were more than 17,000 alarm companies in the United States. Many individuals who run these companies shouldn't be in the business because they are not qualified to do so. It wasn't until recently that states enacted licensing programs to create some form of accountability to protect the consumer.

You won't become a security expert by reading this book. You will, however, become very knowledgeable about alarm systems and be able to make correct decisions for you and your family's security needs. When you complete this book, you will probably know more than the supposed security expert—the salesperson.

Good luck, and have fun getting insight into the fine art of creating your own customized security system.

1 How Does An Alarm Work?

LET'S HAVE A LOOK AT HOW AN ALARM SYSTEM WORKS. Sometimes I am truly amazed at how basic it can be. I think you will be too. You won't need to be an electronics whiz. Just sit back, relax, and be amazed.

First, both commercial and residential alarm systems for the most part work very much alike. The operating theories are identical. In fact, many alarm companies use the same control equipment for both.

The system basically consists of an *alarm master control box* that works on very low voltage, usually about 6 to 12 volts. The inside of the box looks complex, but it's really very simple. The wires come out of the control box, go around the interior of the building, and then back into the control box. This is commonly referred to as the *protection loop* or *alarm circuit*.

Simple so far, right? Wrong. It gets a little more complicated now. To make the master control box activate an alarm, *detection devices* are connected to that protection loop that goes around the inside of the building. These devices are wired in such a way that when they are triggered, the alarm master control box will sense this and activate the alarm system. Usually a loud bell or siren will be attached to the control as well as some type of central-station monitoring. (We'll look at individual devices and how they work in Chapter 2.)

To make things simple, think of the alarm master control box as a water source such as an ocean and the wires that loop around the inside of the building as a long, continuous river. The water flows out of the ocean and into the river, which does what? Right, flows around and back into the ocean again. An alarm basically works the same way. As an example, see Figure 1.

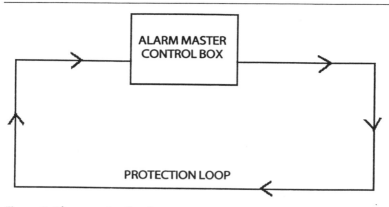

Figure 1. Alarm protection loop.

The alarm control box activates when the flow of low-voltage current that runs through the wiring around the building is interrupted by one or more of the detection devices. To make this clear, let's look at another example. Imagine that the wiring that loops around the inside of a particular building is a water pipe. If we place a shut-off valve on the pipe and close the valve, the water won't be able to complete the loop. Simple, right? Right. But rather than water current running through a pipe, electric current runs through the wiring, which goes around the perimeter of the building. Detection devices are connected individually to the loop in various configurations, each having the ability to interrupt the power flow back to the control. A steady flow of current going out of the control and returning will not activate the alarm. However, if the wiring is cut or one of the detection devices connected to that wiring loop is activated, it is just like turning off a shut-off valve. The alarm master control box senses a loss of power in the wiring loop, and this trips a relay, which activates an alarm.

To review briefly, the low voltage goes out of the master control box and runs through the wires around the interior of the building and back to the control box. Detection devices are connected to that wiring loop. If they sense any problem, they act as a shut-off valve, which prevents the low voltage from going back to the control box. What happens? Since the control box senses a break in the flow, it activates and creates lots of bells and whistles. If the system is monitored, a signal will be sent to the alarm company monitoring station.

It is so simple that if you're having a problem following the theory, you may be wanting to believe it's more difficult than it really is. This chapter is important because the other chapters are built on it. If you feel somewhat lost at this point, please review it again. As you read, the light bulb in your head will turn on as to how simple this all really is.

A word about safety. I recommend that you not attempt any of the following circumvention techniques unless you have been professionally trained in the area of electricity. If you touch the wrong wires, you can be injured. Please keep in mind that the only intention of this book is to explain how alarm systems work so you can develop a more secure system for yourself.

2 Detection Devices

CONTACT SWITCHES

CONTACT SWITCHES ARE THE MOST FREQUENTLY USED PIECES OF alarm detection equipment and, interestingly, are the easiest to circumvent. They are typically applied to movable doors and windows in both homes and businesses. They come in many shapes and sizes and are available in various colors, though the most common are gray or brown.

The contact switch consists of a switch and a magnet. You guessed it—when properly aligned, the magnet holds the switch closed. In Figure 2, the switch is being held together by the magnet that is placed directly below it. In Figure 3, the switch is in the open position because the magnet is no longer there to hold it together.

The most popular type of contact switch can be seen in almost any business that has an alarm system. They are almost always found on the doors of the establishment to detect any illegal entry during closed hours. These are called *surface mount switches* because they are mounted on the inside surfaces of the door and door frame. The switch is mounted on the door or window frame, and the magnet is placed on the movable part of

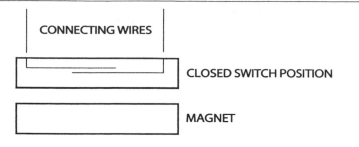

Figure 2. Closed magnetic contact switch.

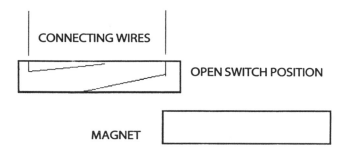

Figure 3. Open magnetic contact switch.

the door or window. If the door or window is opened, the magnet will no longer be in the proper position to hold the switch closed. This will open the switch, which breaks the flow of current to the control box, which in turn trips a relay and sets off the alarm.

Even though the most popular type of contact switch is surface-mounted, they also are available in a recessed version that is actually embedded in the door or window frame and hidden from view (see Figure 4). You typically find these in homes where the aesthetics are important. Most people are very sensitive to any kind of alarm wiring showing in their homes, which makes the recessed switch an ideal choice.

Contact switches are manufactured in various sizes and strengths, depending on the application. The size of the magnet generally corresponds to the strength. The

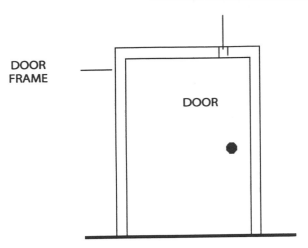

Figure 4. Recessed contact switch mounted in door frame.

bigger the magnet, the stronger it is; conversely, the weaker magnets tend to be small. Whether large or small, the application dictates the size and strength used. For example, the older the door or window that the contact switch is applied to, the more play it usually has. If there is too much play and the magnet strength is not adequate to compensate for the movement in the door, false alarms could result. On the other hand, if the gap between the door and door frame is relatively small, a lighter-duty contact switch would be acceptable.

Contact switches are placed in the protection loop of the alarm system and act as the faucets that we described in the first chapter. When the magnet is holding the switch closed, the electricity is able to flow freely through the protection loop and back to the alarm master control box. However when the magnet is moved away, the switch opens and the electricity can no longer flow through the protection loop and back to the master control. This causes it to activate the bell or siren and, if the system is connected to a monitoring facility, alert the authorities.

Now the fun begins. Here is the 10-second circumvention technique. You won't believe how simple it is to circumvent this very popular and widely used device. Keep in mind that the contact switch is a vital part of almost every alarm system ever installed. Even though this device is one of the simplest to defeat, it is still widely used.

Circumventing a contact switch is as simple as twisting two wires together. In fact, most of the circumvention techniques that we will look at involve twisting only two wires together. The question is, which two? In the case of the contact switch it's easy, because there are only two wires going to the switch.

To completely remove that particular switch from the alarm protection loop, make sure that the alarm is off. If it is on, you will activate it by performing the following procedure.

At this point you may wonder how someone with ill intent could gain access to your system while it is off. A common method of accomplishing this task is called the "inside job." No big mystery how this name came about. The most recent crime statistics show that employee theft is one of the biggest risks to an employer. When someone on the inside sets up an alarm system for a later attack, it can normally be done without being detected easily. The person usually knows interior traffic patterns as well as the general work habits of the other employees, which aids in the act of circumvention not being discovered. Bypassing the alarm can also take place in a busy environment—if a merchant were distracted by a partner in crime, the circumvention could probably be accomplished successfully.

The same holds true for devious relatives who have had their selfish eyes on the family fortune. A home can be set up as easily as a business. Keep an eye on the in-laws. Do you know where your children are tonight? Repair people as well as other visitors could also be setting you up.

Now to the technique. Simply remove the two wires connected to the top of the switch. Strip off some of the insulation or any protective coatings so that the bare wire is exposed. Under normal conditions, only 6 to 12 volts DC run through the wires, so you won't get a shock by touching them. Now twist them together tightly and leave disconnected from the contact switch. By doing

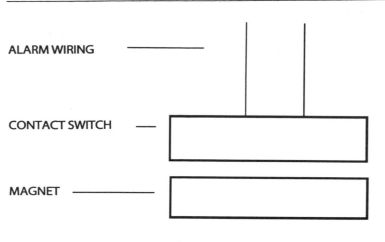

Figure 5. Normal contact switch.

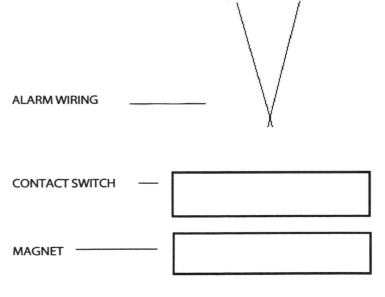

Figure 6. Circumvented contact switch.

this, the alarm protection loop will not see the opening and closing of that particular switch. Why? As far as the alarm master control knows, the system is operating properly because it will receive voltage whether the switch is opened or closed. Since the contact switch is no longer connected to the protection loop, the master control does not see it.

Look at Figures 5 and 6. In Figure 5, you see the contact switch connected properly. In Figure 6, it has been bypassed. This technique is so simple it's amazing that more systems haven't been circumvented this way.

This technique will address 99 percent of all typical alarm systems. There are a few situations where contact switches, when shorted as described above, will actually cause the alarm to activate. However, since the system is off, you will not be detected.

The lesson here is to always conceal all wiring and contact switches when installing an alarm in your home or business. In most cases, surface-mount contacts can be installed in such a way that the wires are hidden in the window and door frames (the recessed version mentioned earlier). This will discourage tampering of your system.

MOTION DETECTORS

Other types of detection devices can be added to the protection loop to enhance the security of your home or business. Let's have a look at the five most popular types of motion detectors.

Infrared motion detectors are the most widely used in security today. They are usually passive detectors, which means that they simply observe an area and don't emit anything. They are the most frequently used motion detectors due to their low false alarm rate, reliability, and sound overall technology. They look like small plastic boxes (see Figure 7) and can usually be found in high foot-traffic locations in homes such as hallways or stairways. In commercial applications, they are often found

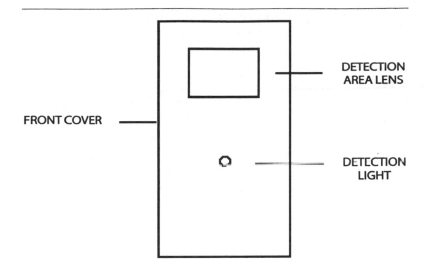

Figure 7. Motion detector.

covering long hallways, warehouses, office areas, or long rows of windows.

Motion detectors are primarily used as backup protection. Why? Simple. Perimeter door and window protection contact switches cannot detect roof or wall entries. Contact switches are great for protecting movable openings, but what if someone knew that the perimeter system was set and that there were no motion detectors inside? They would be able to cut through the door or window or enter through the roof or wall completely undetected because the contact switch would not sense the entry due to the fact that the door or window was not actually opened.

Remember that the perimeter-protecting contact switch needs to be separated from the magnet in order to stop the flow of power back to the alarm master control and activate the alarm. If the door or window isn't actually opened, then the contact switch is worthless in this application. As you can see, the value of motion detectors as backups is great.

The infrared motion detector is designed to activate

when it senses a change of temperature in a room. Every item in the room radiates a certain amount of infrared energy, or heat level. When there is a change in that energy level, such as a person entering the protected area, the infrared detector senses this and opens an internal switch, interrupting the flow of electricity (which is very similar to the way the contact switch operates). And when the internal switch opens, what happens? It acts like someone turned off the faucet, preventing the electricity from getting back to the alarm master control, which activates the alarm.

These devices are manufactured in various configurations that provide various protection patterns as well as protection feet. For instance, if you needed to protect a large warehouse, you might think about using a motion detector designed to cover that large of an area. An office with a small amount of interior space to cover would require a less expensive short-range unit.

Take a moment and go through this exercise with me. Hold your hand directly in front of you by extending your arm forward and reaching out with all five fingers as far as you can. (Why aren't you doing this? Let's go! Right now! Please?) This extension is similar to how an infrared motion detector works. Pretend that your hand is actually the unit and the extended fingers are the pattern of the protection area. In other words, this pattern could be referred to as a "five finger" detection pattern. If an intruder were to walk into a protected area and pass through one of those invisible infrared fingers, the device would detect that individual and activate the alarm master control.

Most motion detectors, including infrared units, are designed to operate in open areas. This means that they cannot see through walls or other obstructions. Consequently, if you are using a long-range detector in a large warehouse, constant caution must be taken in placement of large pieces of inventory and equipment. If a truck or forklift is parked in front of an infrared motion detector, it could block the unit's coverage and create a false sense of security. In a residential application, something as simple as placing a bag of groceries in front of a motion detector can prevent it from doing it's job. That's why we see these detectors mounted in hallways of homes at about a 5-foot height and in commercial buildings at 6 to 8 feet.

The question always comes up for us pet lovers out there: "Won't my dog or cat activate the motion detector?" The answer is both yes and no. I'm a big help, right? But please see Figures 8 and 9.

In Figure 8, we see what might be considered a *plain-wrap* conventional protection pattern. In Figure 9, we have an example of a *pet alley* protection pattern. There are specific models of infrared motion detectors that can be used to create this pet alley. They can be adjusted in such a way that the dog, cat, or other four-legged creature can move freely through the protected area.

You're probably wondering how this is possible. Actually, there is no magic involved. The protection pat-

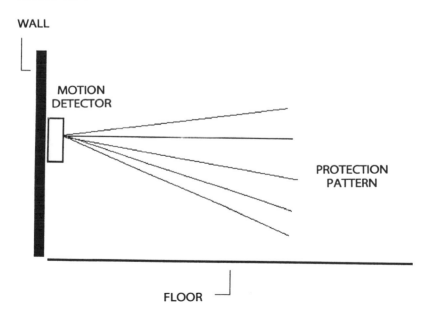

Figure 8. Motion detector sample protection pattern.

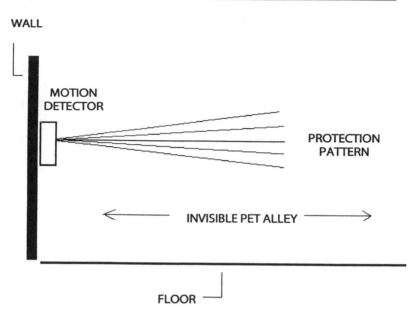

WALL

MOTION
DETECTOR

PROTECTION
PATTERN

← INVISIBLE PET ALLEY →

FLOOR

Figure 9. Motion detector sample protection pattern with pet alley.

tern simply is adjusted to operate on a higher path. This means that the height of the pattern is set to operate about 3 feet or more above the ground. This allows the little darlings to run freely below the protection path without being detected.

Well, at least that's how it's supposed to work. There still needs to be a great deal of caution exercised here. If you're directing the beam down a hallway of your home, for instance, the application will work fine. On the other hand, if you try to create a pet alley in a family room that is full of furniture, you may be asking for false alarms. Why? Simple. In case you didn't already know it, as soon as you leave the house in the morning to go to work, your little four-legged friends jump in your favorite chair for a nice day's rest. What just happened? When Rover jumped on the couch for a nap, he probably jumped higher than what the pet alley would allow. Bingo, he just activated the alarm. The same is true when Muffy takes a wild leap in the air to try to kill that flying bug that has caught her eye.

The whole idea here is to use caution when using the pet alley application. It needs to be pointing in the correct direction and in a clear area away from anything that your pet could get up on.

Look for motion detectors the next time you go to the cleaners, a restaurant, or a friend's home that is equipped with a security system. They almost always have a little red light on the front to show that they are operating properly when someone walks past the unit. It is commonly referred to as the *walk test light*. They really come in handy for both identifying motion detectors and testing if they operate properly.

What, another circumvention technique? Yes! Actually, there are two circumvention techniques for infrared motion detectors. The easiest way to get past one is to cover it or point it away from the area that you want to access. Cover the unit with just about anything that it can't see through, including a cardboard box placed over it, cardboard taped to its front, thick cloth, wood, underwear, etc. Get the picture? If you choose this method, the detector will only see as far as the obstruction and no further. Obviously, this needs to be done when the system is off or else the detector will do its job and detect you and cause a bell or siren to sound.

A little cautionary note. A couple of the motion detector manufacturers have begun to realize that this could be a problem and are beginning to build units that sense blockage. If these are blocked, the detectors will go into an alarm condition, which prevents the system user from being able to set the alarm. Don't let this be a major concern, as most of the detectors on the market today don't have this feature.

The second way to circumvent a motion detector is to think of it as a door or window contact. Do you remember how we circumvented that switch? All of the devices on the protection loop work pretty much alike,

---

and a motion detector is no different. When it senses motion, it activates a small relay, which I'll refer to as a switch inside the detector. Like a contact switch, the motion detector switch operates like a faucet or valve, cutting off the flow of voltage to the alarm master control unit. The master control senses this voltage drop and activates the alarm.

The big question in this situation is which two wires to strip the insulation off of and twist together, because there are four wires usually going into this device. Don't be nervous; this is still a relatively simple procedure.

Remove the cover of the motion detector. It may or may not be held on by a screw. In most cases the plastic cover just pops off with a little pressure (tells you a little something about the alarm industry—cheap, cheap, cheap). This, of course, needs to be done while the system is off or else you will activate the alarm.

Two of the wires that you see will be the voltage wires and two will be the alarm circuit wires. The power terminals inside the motion detector should be marked 6VDC or 12VDC. VDC means *voltage direct current*. DO NOT REMOVE THESE VOLTAGE WIRES! Why? No, you won't get a shock. Rather, the master control will sense no power and the alarm user will not be able to set the system, which creates a service call to the alarm company and your deed will be discovered.

The next step is to remove the two wires that are not connected to the power, strip back the insulation, and, as with contact switches, simply twist them together. Congratulations, you have just learned how to circumvent another very popular security device. It looks like it still works because the power is still connected to the detector. The walk-test light will function properly, and no one will know the difference.

Just for the fun of it, the next time you are in a home or business that is equipped with a motion detector, try to outsmart it. How? If you move very very slowly, I mean a snail's pace, you may be able to walk directly up to the unit without activating it. This is because infrared detectors are designed to give the best coverage if they are cross-walked, that is, to walk across the protection pattern rather than directly into it. Face the detector from about 20 feet away and walk toward it. You may have better success approaching it this way rather than going across the protection pattern or protection fingers.

Ultrasonic motion detectors are also designed to detect motion. Unlike the infrared detector that simply sits on the wall and looks at an area, the ultrasonic motion detector transmits and receives high-frequency sound waves that are extremely difficult for humans to hear. In fact, it's virtually impossible with the later models. The sound is emitted from the transmitter and accepted into the receiver (the newer units are usually referred to as *ultrasonic transceivers* because they transmit and receive out of the same device). When anyone enters the protected area and disrupts the sound pattern, the detector activates the alarm master control and the alarm is set off.

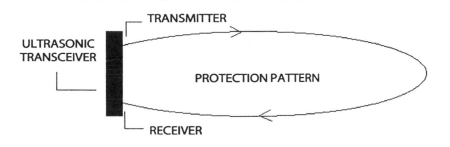

Figure 10. Ultrasonic transceiver.

Ultrasonic motion detectors are no longer considered to be state of the art. Just because they're not being currently installed, however, doesn't mean they are not in use. You'll find many thousands of these detectors still being used in old alarm installations that have not been updated.

The circumvention technique is the same as for the

infrared detector. You should see four wires. Simply identify the power wires and remember not to disconnect them. Remove the other two wires that connect to the alarm loop. Strip back about an inch of insulation and twist together tightly. That's it! You're done. Simple? You bet. Now this detector will no longer be connected to the alarm protection loop, but because you did not disconnect the power wires, the walk-test light will still function as if it were operating and connected perfectly.

Microwave motion detectors were popular at one time for protecting very large areas. As with ultrasonic detectors, microwave units create a protection pattern. If anything or anybody moves in the protected area, the detector senses this and activates its small internal relay tied into the protection loop, which in turn activates the alarm master control.

The main reason that microwave motion detectors are now rarely used is because it is very difficult to control the microwave patterns. The other motion detectors have protection patterns that are contained easily within the protected area by the walls and glass in the room. Microwaves are simply not controllable in this manner because they actually penetrate walls and glass. See Figure 11.

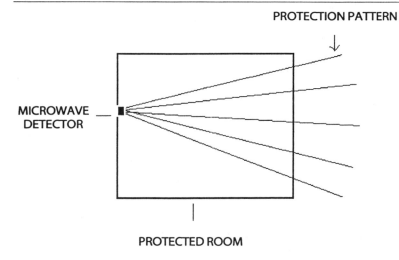

Figure 11. Microwave motion detector pattern.

When this happens, you've probably guessed it—many false alarms. Microwave detectors were seeing cars and people going down the street that were out of the protected area. Obviously this is not acceptable because of the false alarm problem that's created.

Almost all microwave devices have been replaced with more modern technology for alarm applications. You occasionally still see these units in service as the detection device that opens doors at the supermarket.

Photoelectric beams are another form of motion detection . . . sort of. Sort of? This type of motion detector is somewhat different from the rest. You have probably seen many forms of them and not known it. An example would be the annunciation device used in commercial establishments to let the proprietor know when someone has walked in the front door. My dry cleaner happens to have one of these. Most are nothing more than a set of photoelectric detectors hooked into a control and a buzzer.

The detector itself is quite a simple device consisting of a transmitter and a receiver. The transmitter emits a beam of light that is sent to the receiver. The light in the older models is quite visible; the newer models, however, use more of an invisible source and are virtually impossible to see. Please see Figures 12, 13, and 14 for the various photoelectric protection patterns.

When the photoelectric receiver no longer sees the source of light, it opens its internal switch and signals an alarm. This is done very quickly. A break in the light source for as little as a second will trigger an activation of the alarm system. So, guess what happens when an intruder walks into the invisible beam of light? You guessed right—the beam of light is broken and sensed by the receiver, which activates a small switch inside the unit and causes a break in the protection loop. The alarm master control senses this and, yes, the alarm system activates all of the bells and whistles that are attached to it.

This type of detection device is designed to operate over both short and long distances. Some models are designed to go a few hundred feet and some a few thousand. They are primarily used in two applications. The first is a large warehouse situation where a motion detector simply would not reach far enough. For instance, if you were trying to protect a long row of roll-

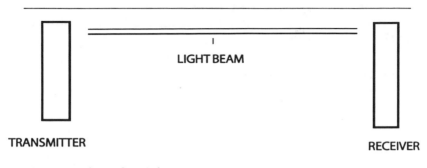

Figure 12. Photoelectric beam.

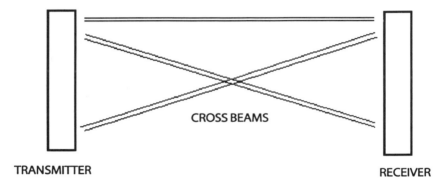

Figure 13. Photoelectric cross beams, type 1.

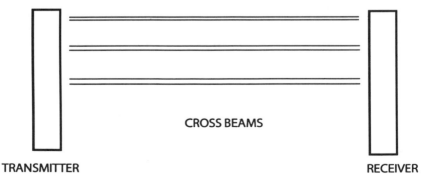

Figure 14. Photoelectric cross beams, type 2.

up doors or a long aisle in a trucking company building, a photoelectric detector could be used to send an invisible beam across the entire length for excellent protection at a minimum price.

The second application might be in an outdoor area such as a car dealer lot or an open storage yard. Outdoor units generally are placed in special enclosures that are tamper-resistant and equipped with small heaters so that the cover of the detector does not fog up or collect morning dew. What I mean by tamper-resistant is that the unit may have a small *tamper switch* connected to the alarm master control that will sound an alarm when the cover is removed. If the detector is so equipped, it is normally in operation only when the alarm system is on.

Now we're ready for the fun part. Circumventing is fairly simple. Let's review. We have two units to be concerned with—the transmitter and the receiver. Since the transmitter normally only transmits light, we don't need to be concerned with it at this time. The receiver, on the other hand, is where the critical pair of wires are. As in the other circumvention techniques, the system needs to be in the off position.

The key is to identify which unit is the transmitter and which is the receiver. Not a difficult task. Look at both units. The transmitter is probably only going to have one pair of wires running into it. That pair is used to power the light source. On the other hand, the receiver should have four wires running into it—two wires for power and two going to the protection loop. It may also have a meter or monitor light on the front to let the service technician or alarm user know whether it is working or not.

As with the other motion detectors that we've previously looked at, you must identify the two wires for power and the two for the alarm loop connection. You don't want to disturb the power wires. Instead, you want to carefully disconnect the pair that connect to the alarm protection loop. Strip back about an inch of insulation and simply twist the wires together. Don't forget to replace the cover. All done.

It's out of service, but since the power is still connected, it will look like it's operating perfectly.

Pressure mats are another form of motion detector. Pressure mats consist of a series of metal strips sandwiched between two sheets of plastic. The strips are wired together in such a way that when pressure is placed on them, they touch and send a signal to the alarm master control to activate the system. They are normally held apart by a spongy type of material (see Figures 15 and 16). The strips themselves are made from

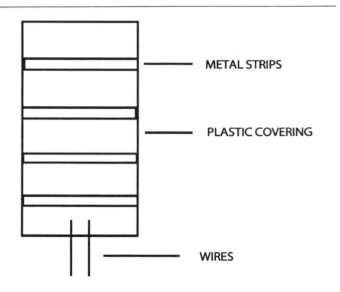

METAL STRIPS

PLASTIC COVERING

WIRES

Figure 15. Pressure mat, top view.

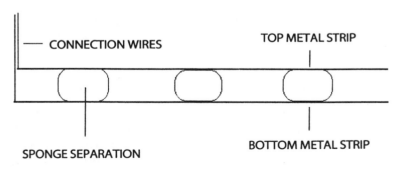

CONNECTION WIRES

TOP METAL STRIP

SPONGE SEPARATION

BOTTOM METAL STRIP

Figure 16. Pressure mat metal strips, side view.

thin pieces of metal that tend to bend and not operate properly when heavy loads are rolled over them.

Pressure mat is purchased by the alarm company on a roll so they can cut off as large a section as needed for your particular application. The price of pressure mats is lower than the other motion detectors, which prompted many alarm companies to sell large quantities of them in previous years.

Pressure mats are more commonly found in homes rather than businesses. In some homes, you can feel the crinkling of plastic under the hallway carpeting. You can bet there is a pressure mat under there.

Pressure mats are naturally good in some locations and poor in others. They are best placed under the carpet in a high foot-traffic location. In a residential application, they are almost always located in the hallway because it is a great central high-traffic location through which most burglars will travel. Burglars seem to always eventually head for the master bedroom, where all the jewelry and other seemingly valuable items are kept.

One drawback to pressure mats is pets. The mat is designed to activate if someone walks on it. Well, if you have a large dog or playful cat, this could be false-alarm city. Pets frequently become a little rambunctious and play hard, especially when no one is home. Salespeople have been known to continue to sell the devices even though technically they shouldn't when pets are present. You should know exactly what you're getting.

Pressure mats are by far the easiest of all devices to circumvent. Unlike the other detectors, in most cases they are considered *open-circuit* devices. All of the other detection devices looked at thus far are *closed-circuit* devices. (Open-circuit devices are those that are considered to be normally open. This means that when the relay is in the open position, the device will not be in an alarm condition. If the device were to close its relay, then it would report an alarm. Conversely, closed-circuit devices are those that are considered to be normally closed. If the normally closed device

---

were to open its relay, then it would report an alarm. Almost all detection devices are designed to operate in a closed-circuit manner to protect the integrity of the alarm system. A wire on an open-circuit system could be cut and no detection would take place, but if a wire were cut on a closed-circuit system, the detection would take place immediately.)

Once you have located the pressure mat, you will see a pair of wires going to it. Simply cut *one* of the wires and the job is complete. It couldn't be easier. In fact, it is so simple that you can cut the wire even if the system is set.

My personal favorite motion detector for the home or business is the infrared motion detector because of its low false alarm rate, reliability, and controllability. If you have a pet situation to overcome, I would recommend using the infrared device and simply direct it over the animals in question. As we discussed earlier, this is known as creating a pet alley.

GLASS-BREAK SENSORS

Glass-break sensors are available in a variety of shapes and sizes. Here are the most common methods of detecting glass breakage.

Audio glass-break sensors are placed in a room next to the area to be protected. They are designed to hear the high-pitched sound of shattering glass. Some units are sensitive enough to cover an entire bank of windows. The disadvantage of using this type of device is that if it is too sensitive, it could hear a noise that may sound like glass breaking and activate the alarm. (More on false alarms in Chapter 10.) Since most of these devices have adjustments built into them, you'll want to test the sensitivity carefully.

In a home, the only protection that is normally used are contact switches attached to the doors and windows and possibly a motion detector in a high-traffic location. Up to this point we have not done anything to physically protect the glass. You can add a motion detector to each room of your home, but due to the cost and inconvenience, that probably isn't a good option.

The audio glass-break sensor is better because it is relatively inexpensive and won't restrict movement in the home the way a motion detector will. Audio glass-break sensors are used to protect businesses too.

Shock sensors are placed on the actual metal frame of a window and are designed to detect the shock of intrusion through that particular opening. There are some new models that act as combination shock sensors and audio units. They come in various sizes, from as small as a quarter up to the size of half a pack of cigarettes.

Shock sensors are mostly used in businesses and are mounted directly on the metal frame of a bank of windows. In Figure 17 you can see where the sensor is located on a typical storefront window. See if you can spot them the next time you're running errands.

The circumvention technique used on shock sensors is the same as with other motion-detection equipment. The two wires that connect to the alarm loop need to be removed from the device and twisted together. That will prevent the unit from being detected on the alarm loop and sending the signal back to the master control.

Window foil is another widely used device to detect glass breakage. You've all seen this stuff. It looks like silver metal tape that is applied to the doors and windows

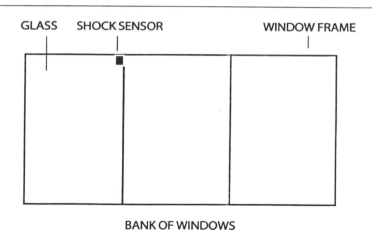

Figure 17. Shock sensor on window frame.

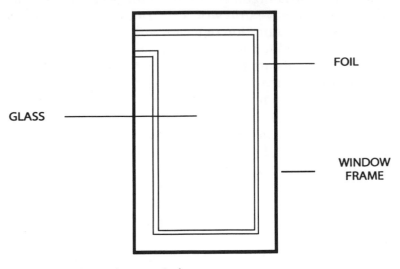

FOIL

GLASS

WINDOW
FRAME

Figure 18. Foil on a door or window.

of commercial buildings. Take a look at the example of a glass door or window protected with foil in Figure 18.

The foil is designed to go around the perimeter of the window, and it is always applied on the inside of the glass. The theory here is simple. The foil acts as if it were a wire protecting the window. When the window is smashed, the foil is broken by the falling glass. Because it is so thin, it breaks very easily. The flow of power is cut off to the alarm master control and the alarm system activates.

This is obviously so simple that you probably are wondering why every alarm company doesn't use it. For starters, it's very old technology. It is also troublesome by nature. It is also very easy to circumvent.

What are some of the problems with window foil? Since it is so thin, window washers can and do tear it very easily. When that happens, the alarm service person needs to stop by and do what is called a *foil repair*, which is really just patching up the tear in the foil. It does have a protective coating on it, but as it ages this coating disappears. Another problem is as the weather changes, the glass contracts and expands slightly. In cold weather it tends to expand and in the heat it contracts. After time, this movement can make small cracks in the window foil, which in turn causes high resistance in the alarm circuit and creates false alarms.

Because of these service problems, foil is not used much anymore on new installations. There are still, however, thousands of windows protected by it.

The circumvention technique for window foil is so simple anyone could do it! Please see Figure 19.

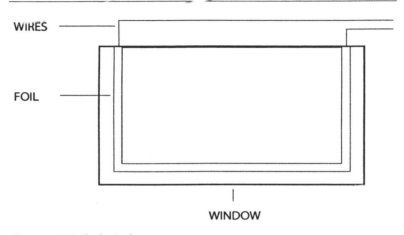

Figure 19. Foiled window.

This is a typical window with foil applied to it. The technique here is almost the same as the others. The goal is to bypass the protection device. As you can see, both ends of the foil are connected to the alarm protection loop. What we do is remove the wires from both sides and twist them together. That's it! The window foil is now out of the protection loop and not capable of sending signals back to the alarm master control because it is now considered to be bypassed, as shown in Figure 20.

The lesson learned in this chapter is that, when designing a security system for your home or business, the placement of detection devices is very important. They need to be placed in an unobstructable area and walk-tested regularly to ensure their proper operation. If

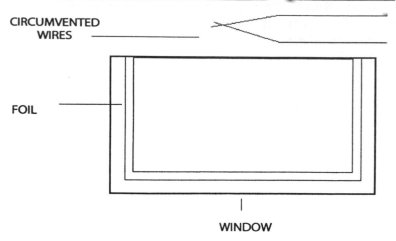

CIRCUMVENTED WIRES

FOIL

WINDOW

Figure 20. Circumvented foiled window.

the motion detectors are walk-tested with the alarm control in the test position, you'll know that they are connected properly to the protection loop and no one has disconnected them because the signals will be acknowledged by the alarm master control. If someone has circumvented the protection loop, the detection signals will not be registering at the master control.

As you noticed while you read through this chapter, almost all of the circumvention techniques are very similar. Contact switches, motion detectors, and other detection devices can be bypassed by simply twisting two wires together. I'm sure you now have a nice secure feeling about your alarm system. Yeah, right! Once again, my purpose in writing this book is not necessarily to show you how to defeat alarm systems but to show you how to protect yourself and your valuables properly.

3 Fire Alarm Systems

FIRE DETECTORS SHOULD BE A PART OF EVERY COMMERCIAL alarm system and a must on all residential applications. There are many types of fire detection devices, which vary with the individual application. We will be looking at the various types of detectors in this chapter.

Due to the fact that fire alarm systems are considered to be lifesaving devices, I will not disclose how to circumvent them. They connect to the protection loop almost the same way as the burglar alarm devices are connected. The difference is that the fire alarms are connected to a separate protection loop in the alarm master control. The reason for this is to differentiate a burglar alarm signal from a fire alarm signal. For instance, if your system is monitored by an alarm monitoring station (we'll review them in Chapter 8), you wouldn't want the fire department to be sent when the burglar alarm is activated. Conversely, you wouldn't want the police to roll to your fire emergency.

Another reason to have a separate protection loop for fire is to provide the option of having a different audible notification. As an example, the burglar alarm's audible signal is normally a warbling type of sound, whereas fire detectors could be set up to provide constant tone. The obvious advantage is to be able to differentiate if the building you're in is in the process of being burned down or burglarized.

Smoke detection devices are very common in homes and businesses. Did you know that all smoke detectors are not the same? Just as the motion detectors described in the previous chapter have different applications, so do smoke- and heat-detection devices.

The typical smoke detector is run by 24 volts, 110 volts, or, in some cases, simply a battery. Many cities and states have enacted ordinances to require installation of such devices in homes. Please believe that smoke detectors really do save lives. If you currently don't have at least one in your home, run, don't walk, to the local hardware store and install it today. Okay? Enough of the lecture.

The most important question for smoke detectors is placement. If you were to have only one smoke detector in your home (although more than one is preferable), I would recommend that it be placed near the sleeping area. After all, it is designed to wake you up and alert you that there is a fire. This location would commonly be a hallway.

The type of detector for use in your home may be different than that used in a business. It has a lot to do with the environmental conditions. In most residential applications, the photoelectric or ionization type of detector is used. This also applies to clean office situations. Why clean? If the detector is allowed to get full of dirt and dust, it will more than likely malfunction and create false alarms. One thing is certain—you want to avoid false fire alarms at any cost. It's not fun to see the street in front of your home filled with fire fighting equipment when it's not necessary for them to be there. It could be extremely embarrassing as well as expensive, as many municipalities are now charging for false alarms.

As previously mentioned, placement is very important. As an example, if a smoke detector is placed too close to a kitchen and the toast burns, big trouble! C... have a false alarm. Another example of incorrect plc... ment would be directly in a bathroom or outside t... bathroom door. The smoke detector could see showe... steam as smoke and go into an alarm condition, which activates the alarm master control and sounds the alarm. So the question becomes: how do I effectively protect these areas?

A *rate-of-rise* or *thermal detector* is a device that uses temperature rather than smoke to activate the fire alarm system. In fact, the protected area could be totally engulfed in smoke but not actually on fire and this detector would not see it at all. I'm sure you'll agree that using the correct detector in the application is very critical.

The rate-of-rise detector is designed to detect a rapid change in heat rise or, depending on the detector, activate at a certain temperature, most commonly 135 or 170 degrees Fahrenheit. This would be good to use in a kitchen, for example, unless it were placed directly over the stove. Get it? Rate of rise.

In a dirty commercial application such as a manufacturing facility, rate-of-rise detectors would be used rather than smoke devices due to the dust and contaminants that may create false alarms and a negative situation with the fire department.

Halon extinguishing systems are found primarily in computer rooms or in areas where one would want a method of extinguishing a fire without the use of water. In a computer or electrical room, the last thing you would want is water flowing out all over the electrical equipment. That could cause some very extensive and costly damage. The Halon system is a fire extinguishing system that uses a smoke detector to sense fire. When it does, it releases a chemical that puts out the fire quickly. No mess, no water. These systems tend to be a bit expensive, but they work remarkably well.

Sprinkler systems are found primarily in commercial buildings and industrial complexes. However, some

s are now requiring systems to be installed in new
nes, condos, and apartment complexes.

In case you haven't figured it out, I'm a big fan of fire
rotection and particularly fond of sprinkler systems. The
reason is that they work very well in extinguishing or con-
trolling fire until the fire department arrives.

How do they work? Simple. When the heat of a fire
raging below a sprinkler head rises up to the ceiling, it
activates that particular head, which sprays water on
the fire in an attempt to extinguish the flames.

A common question arises almost every time the topic
of sprinkler systems arises. Does the entire sprinkler system
pour water on the fire? The answer is definitely no. Only
the sprinkler heads that get hot enough to activate actually
dispense water. As the fire expands in a building, the rest of
the heads spray out water on their areas.

There are several reasons why systems are set up this
way. Maintaining strong water pressure as well as mini-
mizing water damage are at the top of the list. Once a
sprinkler head is activated, the water will continue to
run until it is manually shut off. This is usually done by
the fire department upon arrival.

They can shut it off in many ways. The most common would be either by the *OS&Y valve*, generally
located in the building on the riser pipe that feeds
water to the sprinkler heads. The other shut-off valve
is called a *post-indicator valve* located outside the
building. The post-indicator valve is generally paint-
ed red and looks like a post coming out of the ground.
It is usually about 3 feet tall and serves as the shut-off
valve to all of the water going into the building relat-
ed to the fire system.

Question: Could the water be shut off at the post
indicator valve and completely shut off the sprinkler
system? The answer is yes. However, the alarm industry
has created a tamper switch that would send a signal to
the alarm company when the valve is closed. Obviously,
this is a critical component to the sprinkler system and
needs to be monitored.

If you are occupying a building that is equipped with a sprinkler system, you should consider having monitored by a quality alarm company. Fire detection devices save lives. Please invest in them if you have not already done so. Don't wait until it's too late. It's real ugly!

4 Wireless Alarm Systems

Up to this point, we have looked at how wired alarm systems operate. Now we're going to discuss the wonderful world of wireless security systems.

In the alarm industry, wired systems are commonly referred to as *hard-wired systems*. Wireless systems are simply referred to as *wireless*. The two systems operate in a similar fashion. The difference is that rather than having the alarm activate the master control unit by sending a signal from the protection device to the control through the protection loop, the signal in a wireless system is transmitted back via radio signal. Well, that's how it is supposed to work. Wireless devices have some advantages as well as some significant disadvantages. Let's look at both.

At each detection device (i.e., contact switch, motion detector, etc.), a small wireless transmitter is connected the same way as in a hard-wired system. The transmitters vary in size. Some of the older models are as large as a pack of cigarettes. The newer models, however, are quite compact, about half the size of the older ones. If you were to open a transmitter, you would see a small circuit board with some electronic parts and an antenna. Oh yes, don't forget about the battery. Yes, these

es that are designed to save life and property oper-
on a battery. Feeling safe yet? More about that later.
You will also see a pair of wires coming out of the
ansmitter, or possibly a terminal with two small
crews. This is how the detection devices are connected
to the transmitter. As an example, if we were connecting
a door contact switch to the transmitter, the pair of wires
from the transmitter would connect directly to the two
terminals on the contact switch (see Figure 21). The
same holds true for motion detectors and just about any
other detection device.

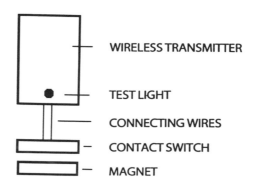

Figure 21. Wireless door/window transmitter connected to a contact switch.

Another type of popular wireless transmitting device
that is used primarily for personal protection is the pendant or belt clip type of push-button signaling device. A
pendant is generally worn around the neck like a coach
would wear a whistle (see Figure 22). It may be used by
individuals who have medical conditions—if they need
help, they simply push the button, a wireless signal is
sent to the alarm master control, a signal is sent to the
monitoring company, and medical help is dispatched.

Another application would be robbery protection.
Occasionally you see employees of high-security businesses such as jewelry stores or gun shops carrying these
units. It, too, may be a pedant or belt clip device that

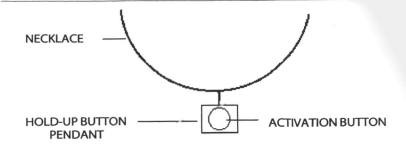

NECKLACE

HOLD-UP BUTTON PENDANT — ACTIVATION BUTTON

Figure 22. Wireless pendant button.

looks like a small garage door opener (see Figure 23). If a holdup attempt is made, the button is pushed and help is on the way. A similar device could be connected to a home alarm system. While the user is in the yard or driving into the driveway, the device could summon help.

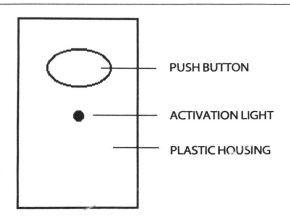

PUSH BUTTON

ACTIVATION LIGHT

PLASTIC HOUSING

Figure 23. Wireless portable button.

Now that we have looked at the various transmitting devices, you may be wondering how the signal is received at the alarm master control panel. Simple! A radio receiver picks up the transmitter signal and activates a relay, which in turn activates the alarm master control. To make things really clear, imagine the hard-e configuration that we looked at earlier and simply place the wired protection loop with an individual ireless link from each detection device to the alarm naster control.

These devices are also known as *short-range wireless equipment*. How short, you ask? As a general rule, 1,000 feet is a good guess, but it really varies because the range is diminished by any obstacles in its path. (Obstructions can diminish the overall range of any type of radio transmitting equipment.) The worst obstacles are things like solid concrete walls, metal, large mirrors, and articles of inventory in a commercial establishment.

So you're probably asking the question, why aren't all systems wireless? Why should alarm installers take all of that installation time to install a hard-wired alarm in my home or business? The wireless system seems as reliable as a hard-wired system, right? Wrong!

Due to the fact that wireless systems transmit the protection device's signal via radio, it is not considered to be as reliable as a hard-wired system. The reason is that radio, by nature, is open to interference by other radios on the same frequency or, worse, high-powered radios interfering with transmission of the signal. Manufacturers have come a long way in developing better transmitters (like some of the new wireless telephones on the market, some features are being built into transmitters to prevent frequency interference), but there are obvious limits when the overall cost comes into play.

Another problem with wireless is that with some systems, you cannot determine if all of the doors and windows are closed when you set the alarm. Obviously important to know, right? This type of system is referred to as a *nonsupervised wireless system*. Many manufacturers are building *supervised systems*. If a door or window is left open when the supervised system is about to be set, you will be notified by a zone indication light or an audible tone and can remedy the situation. Unfortunately, with a nonsupervised system you'd never

---

know and possibly set your alarm with a door o
dow left open. Nonsupervised systems are being ph
out as the supervised technology improves.

Remember that battery that we addressed earli
The wireless transmitter has no other power sourc
Simply speaking, if the battery is dead, the transmitte
will not be able to transmit. Some manufacturers have
improved battery longevity by using a lithium battery
rather than the standard 9-volt model. Additionally,
manufacturers are building in early warning detection
if the battery starts to lose power.

If you changed all of the batteries at one time, you
might think that they would all last about the same
amount of time, right? Wrong! Doors and windows that
are used more than others will use more battery power,
because every time they are opened and closed, the
transmitter is activated, which uses battery power.

There are some advantages to wireless alarm systems. They are simple to install, which cuts down the
installation time considerably. They can be easily
moved to another building since they simply screw
onto the wall. The portable panic and medical features are great, but relying totally on wireless security
is not recommended.

Circumvention can be as easy as removing the battery from the transmitter on some models, removing
one of the wires on the wireless receiver that connects to
the control panel, or simply snipping off the receiving
antenna. Additionally, the twisting together of detection
device wires, as we looked at earlier, is also applicable
on the wireless devices.

If you were to ask the average alarm technician (not
the salesman selling it to you) what he thought about
wireless security systems, the negative answers would
amaze you. Try it!

Chapter

5 Alarm Master Controls

LET ME START BY TELLING YOU THAT THERE ARE LITERALLY hundreds of different alarm master controls on the market. So, how do you know which one to select? As you talk to various alarm companies, you will hear some names of equipment over and over again. This is generally a good indication that that master control is a popular model and will last for some time.

The alarm master control consists of a box with a circuit board as well as a backup battery in case the power should fail or an intruder deliberately turns it off. The battery should be rechargeable so that it will be ready and fully charged when you need it. When selecting an alarm, ask if it comes with this power protection.

The master control is the brain of the alarm system. All of the wiring needs to lead in or out of this box, so its placement is critical. The goal here is to place the control in the most secure place within the protected area. A central closet is the most popular location. Why? If it is centrally located, it is less of a problem when running wire, and the shorter wire runs are useful in saving installation time. Try to keep the actual control box out of sight, too. You'll see why when we look at the circumvention technique.

The main function of the control is to send and receive power to and from the protection loop. Remember how in the first chapter we looked at how the detection devices act as valves turning the flow of electricity on and off in the protection loop? Well, when the alarm control senses that the power is going out and not returning, a series of actions occur. A relay is activated within the unit, which triggers another relay, which turns on an audible device such as a bell or siren. In addition, if the control is equipped with a digital communicator or similar device, the alarm monitoring station will be notified and the police will be dispatched. (More about monitoring stations in Chapter 8.)

One of the best features of the newer alarm controls is the zoning capability. A *zone* is a separate channel of the alarm control that alarm signals can be sent in on. An example would be putting all of the openings of the front of a building on zone 1, the rear on zone 2, and the sides on zones 3 and 4. Perhaps the fire signals will be on another zone and the holdup or medical alarm on another. As you can see, zoning the alarm properly is a giant benefit in quickly determining where the alarm is coming from or what signal is coming in. There are alarm master control units that are expandable to up to 100 zones or more. If you wanted to pinpoint each and every detection device in your home or business, it would be doable with this technology.

The type of *keypad* is another consideration when selecting which alarm equipment to go with. Unfortunately, many people are taken in by the bells and whistles rather than how well the unit will service their needs. A keypad is used to do much more than just turn the alarm system on and off. It can incorporate many features, such as activating a *duress alarm* in the event "the bad guy" follows you to the door and orders you to turn the system off. With most models, you simply put in a duress code and the system will appear to shut down; however, an emergency duress signal is

---

silently transmitted to the alarm company mon... facility. Definitely a recommended feature.

Keypads are generally placed inside the buil... and look basically like a telephone touch pad with audible device and an *LCD* (liquid-crystal display) *LED* (light-emitting diode). The display tells you the con... dition of the system and, in the event of an alarm, what zone has been activated. The audible device will usually make a low-level sound when pushing the keys to let you know it's alive. In the event of an actual alarm, the sound level may increase from the keypad as well as any sirens or bells that are attached to the alarm master control. I recommend that you select a touch pad that is backlit. You'll find this feature beneficial when trying to arm or disarm the system in the dark.

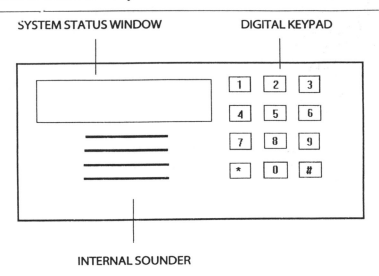

SYSTEM STATUS WINDOW   DIGITAL KEYPAD

INTERNAL SOUNDER

Figure 24. Sample digital keypad.

The location of the keypad is important for convenience and, most important, good security. Number one rule: keep all of the keypads inside the building. In a commercial application, placement on the interior wall near the door that the first employee enters

n in the morning and the last employee leaves
night is probably best. If they are different, then
r use two keypads or place one in a central loca-
between the two entrances.

I know. You're probably thinking, "If the alarm
quipment is inside of the building, including the keypads, how do I enter and exit the building without activating the system?" Well, you have to tolerate the
shrieking sound of the sirens. Just kidding! The alarm
manufacturers have included a feature in the alarm
master control that enables you to enter and exit without activating the system and creating a false alarm. It
is called *entry/exit delay*.

The entry/exit delay is zoneable. This means that
the openings where you wish to have it can be delayed
while all other openings can activate instantly when
someone enters through them. As a recommendation,
the only openings that should be connected to delay
zones are the most frequently used doors to enter and
exit the property.

The time period is adjustable for both the entry and
exit of the protected premises. The exit time is generally
set at about 60 seconds. That means you can go to the
keypad, set the system, and have 60 seconds to proceed
out the door. THIS DOES NOT MEAN 61 SECONDS! Any
longer and the alarm will go into the entry delay period
time, and you will create a false alarm. That's something you don't want to do. (More about false alarms in
Chapter 10.)

The entry delay period works in a similar fashion.
For example, it's time to leave your home and go to
work in the morning. You set the alarm system and
walk out the door. The alarm is now set. You come
home in the evening and put the key in the front door.
The door opens and the alarm doesn't activate. Is it
broken? No. You are experiencing the entry delay period. The alarm will not activate immediately so that
you will have enough time to get to the keypad to turn
the system off.

Sometimes alarm installation companies pro⸱
all entry and exit times the same. They do this si⸱
because it is easier. I recommend that the entry time
set for as little time as possible, probably 15 to 30 se
onds. Just make it convenient; you don't want to have t
rush to turn off the alarm.

There's another reason why the entry delay period
is critical. A burglar will have the amount of time you
have set in the delay to roam around the protected
premise to steal things or possibly circumvent the
alarm system.

I think that proper placement of the keypads in a
home is a little more important because it really
becomes a life-style issue, where family members may
be entering and exiting at all hours of the day and
night. If the system becomes awkward to use, it probably won't be used as much as it should and maybe not
at all. Consider having keypads installed near the door
or doors that are most commonly used.

In addition, it is recommended that a keypad be
placed in the bedroom that you sleep in. I know this
sounds a little odd, but here is why you should consider it. In the event of a burglary when you are sleeping
in your bedroom, you will hear the alarm activate but
wonder where the intrusion has taken place. If you
can access the keypad easily, you could see which zone
has been activated and make a location determina-
tion. If you have a duress or holdup feature, you will
be able to summon the alarm monitoring station from
the keypad. By doing this, they will not only receive
the burglar alarm signal but also a duress signal, letting them know that you are in the building and need
assistance. In some cases, the police may respond
faster to the emergency.

One more feature that is offered on some of the mid-
to high-end security systems is a *direct listen-in feature*.
This allows the alarm monitoring station to listen into
your home in the event the system is activated. In some
systems, the microphone is located in the keypad; in

s, it is installed separate from the keypad in central ~~tions in the building.

The microphones in use today are very good at picking up sounds throughout a home or business. I have seen ~~em manufactured both one-way and two-way. The one-way model allows the monitoring station to listen in only; they cannot talk back to you. The two-way model allows conversation both ways, which is a real benefit if you have a medical problem and need to explain your condition to the monitoring station operator.

I know, I know. I can hear you thinking, "I can't remember a code, and I want to use a key instead." Shame on you! Many of the older systems that have been around 10 years or longer have the key-access type of on/off switch, but in all seriousness, they really aren't very secure.

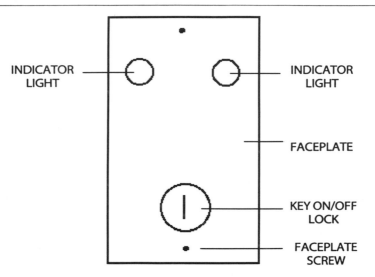

INDICATOR LIGHT

INDICATOR LIGHT

FACEPLATE

KEY ON/OFF LOCK

FACEPLATE SCREW

Figure 25. Keyed on/off control switch.

First of all, you find most of the key on/off devices located on the outside of buildings near the entrance doors. Also, many of the early installations don't have any type of tamper protection on the key lock. That

means that an intruder who knows what to do can
off the entire alarm system by removing the lock
shorting the wires. Remember, even the sophistica
keypads on the market today should not be mounte
outside of the protected area. Why create an invitatior
for anyone to have access to your security system from
the outside of the building?

Okay, this is the highlight of the chapter. The
alarm master control equipment can be circumvented
just like all of the detection devices that we have
reviewed. With the detection devices, however, the circumvention technique assumed that the alarm system
was in the off position while completing the task. This
time, I will describe a quick down-and-dirty technique
to disable the system while it is set and you are outside
the building.

One of the only ways to enter a building without
being detected is to get to the alarm master control
immediately and disable it before the signal can be gen-
erated and sent to the monitoring station. Let's assume
that the alarm system is monitored by a conventional
digital communicator and there are no audible devices
such as bells or sirens connected to the system. Most systems take approximately 20 to 30 seconds to generate
an alarm message to the monitoring station. Okay,
you're probably ahead of me at this point. Simply go
directly to the alarm master control and cut all of the
wires that lead in or out of the box. If you can perform
this task in a timely manner, the conventional alarm
system will become totally inoperative, including all
audible devices and signal transmitting equipment. In
my experience, I have seen these attempts to circumvent alarms work quite well. By the way, the tool of
choice is not a pair of wire cutters—an ax seems to do
the job much better.

Another common question is, "What happens if I
cut the wires to the keypad?" Generally, not much. The
wires run back to the alarm master control, but it still
would be connected to both the protection loop and

.toring station. The alarm master control needs to
.aken out to be effective.

As you can see, the point that we covered earlier
ally hits home now—that is, to have the alarm master
.ontrol located in a secure position in the building that
you want to protect. An ideal situation would be to have
the control equipment in a locked closet with a contact
switch on the door or a motion detector in the closet
connected to an instant alarm zone.

Within the last few years, the alarm industry has
improved the quality of these control devices, and they
have become quite reliable. The decision of which one
to buy will purely be a personal one depending on the
features that you ultimately decide that you really need,
not what the salesperson wants you to have.

Chapter

6 Holdup Devices

As we saw in Chapter 4, "holdup" devices are wireless transmitting units that are used primarily for personal protection or in cases of medical emergencies. One thing that was not thoroughly covered is the most advantageous placement of these devices both residentially and commercially. Placement is a critical topic. Of course, I won't be able to give you specific locations because everyone has different needs and requirements.

To begin, all holdup systems are designed to be silent. The last thing you want to do is have a loud siren activate as you're being robbed. That's a good way to get shot. Don't get confused with *panic alarms* used in residential applications, which are supposed to make noise when the button is activated. If you see someone approaching the back of the house carrying a crowbar and wearing a mask, you would probably want to think about activating the panic alarm to scare this creep away and alert the authorities. A silent alarm wouldn't do too much good here, right?

Both holdup and panic buttons are wired into what's known as a *24-hour circuit* in the alarm master control. That means that even if the burglar alarm system is

ed off, the holdup system will operate 24 hours a
. Well, that's how it's supposed to work.

The next question is when to activate the device.
hat would you do in this scenario. You are at the cash
egister of a mini-market and in walks a man that you
know is wanted for robbing the store down the road last
week. You probably would not be able to call the police
because he would hear you. Would you push the holdup
button? When? There may not be right or wrong
answers to these questions. One thing is certain, however—placement of a holdup device is very critical right
about now! Obviously it wouldn't be wise to allow Mr.
Slime Ball holdup man to see you running across the
room to push a button. I think you can see how important placement can be.

Let's briefly review holdup devices. The two basic
categories are hard-wired and wireless. Both types
have positives as well as negatives. The main advantage of the wireless holdup device is that it is portable
and can be kept with you in your home or business.
Everyone who has a life-threatening medical condition should have one of these to summon help when
they cannot get to a telephone. In my experience,
wireless devices are sold to homeowners in greater
numbers than to businesses.

In commercial applications, the hard-wired device is
most popular for several reasons. The first one that
comes to mind is the fact that it is mounted in the same
place day in and day out, whereas employees tend to
lose the portable wireless devices. Also, many commercial buildings are very large, where wireless devices may
not work due to the lack of frequency range, although in
a small retail operation they should work fine.

The topic of placement is somewhat subjective. In a
commercial operation, ask yourself these questions: if
someone were to hold us up, how would they do it? How
could they enter? Where could they lock us up in the
building? The restroom? The office? The refrigeration
unit? The answer to all of these could be "yes," as these

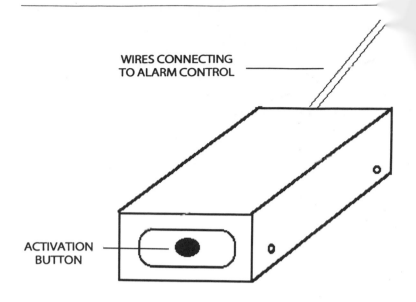

WIRES CONNECTING
TO ALARM CONTROL

ACTIVATION
BUTTON

Figure 26. Hard-wired hold-up button.

are places where victims have actually been held. When you consider placement, be open-minded and creative, no matter how uncomfortable it makes you feel. Take time to be prepared.

The types of applications for wireless alarms are as varied as the devices used to activate the alarm control panel. So far, the holdup button has been the most popular choice. It's relatively simple to use and dependable. But there are other devices that are even better for certain applications. The object here is to be able to alert the monitoring center in the event of a holdup without tipping off the masked man who has a gun in your face that you have activated the system.

In banks, one popular setup is the *foot rail*. It's mounted on the floor at the teller window. During a holdup, the teller slips his or her foot into the device and lifts it up. The signal is sent to the alarm monitoring station. This activation process is very quiet and cannot be detected by the robber.

nother popular device is called a *money clip*. It con-
s of a clip that is mounted in a cash register drawer.
single dollar bill or piece of paper is placed in the
oney clip and remains there. Once the system is set,
he removal of that bill from the clip will activate the
silent holdup alarm. A combination of one or more of
these may be right for your particular application.

I'll bet you thought I was going to close this chapter
without giving you the circumvention technique. The
best and easiest way to disarm a holdup system is to
refer to Chapter 11, "The Ultimate Circumvention
Technique."

7 Audible Devices

WE HAVE ALL HEARD AND CURSED THEM. YOU KNOW, THOSE annoying blaring sirens, those infamous noisemakers that absolutely nobody pays attention to. In this chapter you will learn everything you wanted (or possibly not wanted) to know about these sometimes useful devices.

You see sirens or bells on commercial buildings as well as on homes. Alarm companies place them on the outside as well as on the inside. In this author's opinion, depending solely on a bell or siren for protection simply isn't enough. Why? In most cases, nobody is going to care, much less react to your situation. Alarm monitoring is a better way to go, but more about that in the next chapter.

It seems as though in more current installations, alarm companies are using more sirens than bells. The cost is less, and the siren is much lighter and easier for the installer to handle. On older systems, however, you will notice the ever-familiar rusting bell box mounted on the exterior of the building. See Figures 27 through 32.

There is no specific rule as to where audible devices are supposed to be mounted. There may be one on the

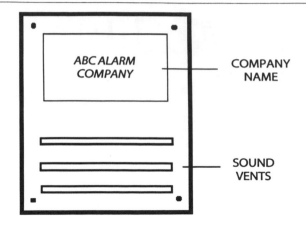

Figure 27. Alarm bell box.

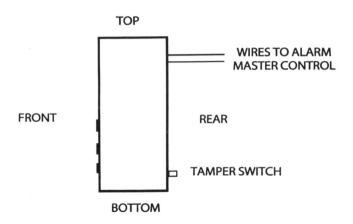

Figure 28. Alarm bell box, side view.

outside of the building or one on the inside, possibly both. The exterior sirens generally are mounted in a metal box on commercial buildings, or in the attic facing out through a vent on homes. The inside sirens can be found anywhere in a commercial building. For some reason, however, I've noticed them mounted very close to the alarm master control. Gee, can you guess why they do that? If you said that it is due to lack of initiative

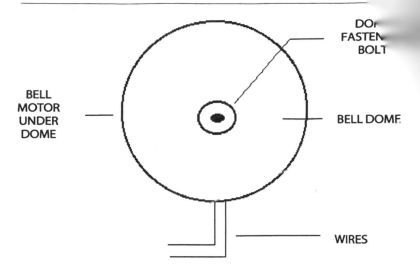

Figure 29. Alarm bell.

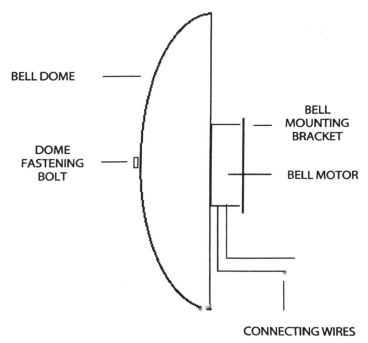

Figure 30. Alarm bell, side view.

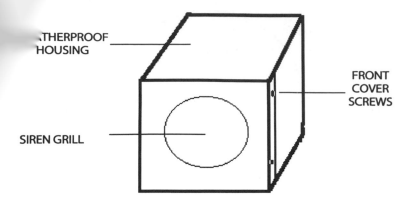

Figure 31. Siren and housing.

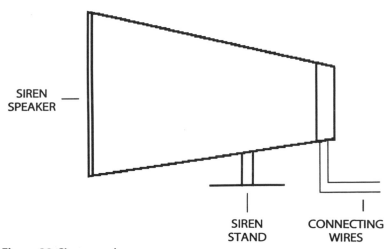

Figure 32. Siren speaker.

and laziness, you get a gold star. By installing the audible device in this manner, the installation company saves time by not having to make a long wire run. As we all know, time is money.

In residential applications, the internal siren is often in the heater air-return vent. In the section on keypads in Chapter 5, we noted that mini noisemakers can be installed in the keypad. In most instances they are merely warning buzzers and really are not designed to scare off a big bad burglar.

Now comes the big event—the 10-second circumvention technique. The alarm system can be on or off when completing this task. Once you have located the bell or siren, you will see two low-voltage wires running into it. Simply cut each wire. Okay, all done! That's all there is to it. The bell or siren can no longer make a noise. It's dead. The beauty of this is that in most cases the audible device is not supervised by the alarm master control in any way. That means that no signals will go to the monitoring station.

One caution—if the exterior device is mounted in a metal box, it will usually have a tamper switch built into it, like the one in Figure 33. If the box is opened or pulled off the wall that it's affixed to, the tamper switch will open and activate the noisemaker right in your hand. No big deal. If this happens, simply cut all of the

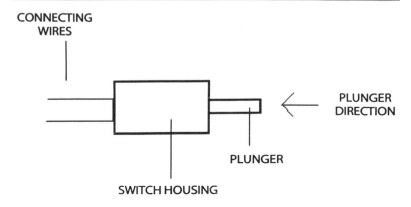

Figure 33. Plunger/tamper switch.

wires that lead to that box, or open the box when the alarm system is off and disconnect at that time. This technique works well with the "ultimate circumvention technique" discussed in Chapter 11.

As in the previous examples, it is really important to keep the audible devices in the building for that extra asure of security. If exterior devices must be used, install them as high as possible to help prevent the possibility of tampering. Make sure that the devices that you choose to make sound, whether they be bells or sirens, are the loudest that are legal in your city. In my opinion, you need to have as much noise as possible to scare away the inexperienced burglar. Even if the neighbors don't respond, the intruder will be thinking that everyone is watching and detection has taken place. The more noise you can create, the more disoriented and fearful the burglar will be. With some luck he will leave immediately.

Chapter

8

Alarm Monitoring

In the previous chapters we have touched upon the topic of alarm monitoring stations. Monitoring is a feature that is well worth having, provided you have the right people doing the job. Let's take a look at the nuts and bolts of what that's all about.

An alarm monitoring station is a facility that monitors alarm systems. No surprise, right? Wrong! Read on. The monitoring facility may be located in your city. On the other hand, it could be located across the country. If you currently have a monitored alarm system, do you know where it is monitored? Have you stopped by to see the facility? Unfortunately, most alarm system owners really don't take the time to find out where their signals are going. This is important, because when a crisis occurs, it's too late to be addressing these issues.

Monitoring facilities fall under two categories: those listed by Underwriter Laboratories (a private organization that tests electronic equipment) and those not listed by Underwriter Laboratories. The listed facilities undergo inspections on a fairly regular basis and need to meet certain requirements set forth by Underwriter Laboratories. The list of the requirements are too numerous to mention in this chapter, but their purpose is to create a

...ard of installation and monitoring performance. ...is not to say that non-UL-listed monitoring facilities ...not as good. In fact, many are as good, if not better, ...an their listed counterparts.

There are numerous reasons why it is important to see the alarm monitoring station before you ultimately choose it. The most important is that you will know where the facility is as well as what it looks like. I know this will sound a little strange, but I have seen some companies monitor alarm systems from the most interesting places. How about a spare bedroom of the house, for instance, with family members taking turns 24 hours a day monitoring the incoming signals. Or from a basement. Don't laugh. In this modern world of technology, I've seen both. Surprised? Don't be. The alarm industry tends to be highly segmented. Therefore this type of thing can occur.

Now, go to the phone and call your alarm company and make an appointment for a tour. See how it looks. Is it a secure building? Do the employees look like they can walk and chew gum at the same time? After all, these people will have a significant effect on your life should you need them.

Today's modern monitoring facilities can really look like space control centers. They are very high tech, with special lighting so that the operators who respond to your signals will not suffer from tired eyes or fatigue. These state-of-the-art monitoring centers are fully automated by sophisticated computers and software programs.

When the alarm master control activates in the home or business, the message is transmitted to the monitoring station. See Figure 34 for a simplified alarm monitoring screen. The automation system will determine whether it is an emergency or a routine signal. If it is an emergency, the proper agency is notified and help is on the way. If a fire signal comes in, of course the fire department will be sent. If an intrusion signal is received, then the police will be dispatched.

```
┌─────────────────────────────────────────────────┐
                    ABC COMPANY
                    1234 ANY STREET
                    ANYCITY, LM 12345

   ALARM ZONE    [ 2 ]    FIRE ALARM—FRONT OFFICE

   CALL LIST:
     MR. BUSINESSMAN, (205) 123-1234
  ─────────────────────────────────────────────────
                   SPECIAL INSTRUCTIONS
  ─────────────────────────────────────────────────
   SEND FIRE DEPARTMENT, (205) 123-4567
   NOTIFY FIRE DEPARTMENT THAT KEYS ARE IN THE KNOX BOX
     BY FRONT DOOR
   NOTIFY MR. BUSINESSMAN ON ANY ALARM
└─────────────────────────────────────────────────┘
```

Figure 34. Simplified sample screen from a monitoring computer.

To transmit signals to the alarm monitoring facility, the system needs to be equipped with a device known as a *digital communicator*. It is standard equipment in many alarm master controls in existence today. The digital communicator transmits the signal to the monitoring station via telephone line. The signal consists of bits of information that are read by the receiving equipment in the monitoring company. It is then displayed to the live dispatcher or operator, and action is taken.

9 The "Business" of the Alarm Business

JUST BECAUSE YOU SEE A LARGE ADVERTISEMENT IN THE Yellow Pages doesn't mean that you're looking at a large company. In fact, in many cases the opposite is true. Many of the larger, more established companies run smaller advertisements. They are better known and therefore don't feel that they need to invest so much money on telephone book advertising.

Please allow me to let you in on a little secret. There are approximately 17,000 alarm companies in the United States, and approximately 20 percent or less own their own monitoring facilities. Surprised? You're probably wondering why there are so few compared to the number of dealers who install alarms. The message is clear that a majority of the alarm companies out there share central monitoring stations.

In the last chapter we looked at how segmented this business really is. This situation has spawned a complete new business—the business of monitoring for small companies that choose not to invest in their own monitoring stations. These companies do no installations; they are solely in the business of monitoring alarm systems nationwide from an ultramodern state-of-the-art facility capable of handling thou-

of alarm systems from one central location. sometimes.

Ready for more interesting news? The alarm installation companies that use these monitoring stations pay a rate, which ranges anywhere from $5 to $10 per month depending on the type of services required for the particular customer. The installation companies also get special rates in many cases, depending on how many of their customers are being monitored.

Now let's do some simple arithmetic. The average homeowner pays the alarm company anywhere from $18 to $30 per month. If you're paying $25 per month for monitoring and the alarm company is paying their contract central station only $5, obviously the alarm company is earning $20 per month from you in profits. Not bad! In some instances, however, the installation company will provide system service, which is also included in the monthly fee. It's like an extended warranty. As long as you're paying the monthly monitoring fee, the installation company will service the alarm for you should anything go wrong with it. It is something you want to ask for.

So what is the big deal whether or not the alarm provider actually owns their own monitoring facility? It is strictly my personal opinion, but I strongly feel that the local alarm company has more control over what happens in an emergency situation than the long-distance contract monitoring services.

In many markets in the United States, you can see and hear advertisements on radio and television touting alarm systems for a very low installation fee, in many cases at or below cost. Why? All together now . . . for the monthly fees that those low installation prices can produce. In the long run, this can be quite lucrative for the installation companies. Large companies can sell as many as 1,000 alarm systems per month. More arithmetic. One thousand new systems sold a month at a monthly monitoring fee of $20 amounts to a lot of money—$20,000 per month in new revenue. As you can

see by this example, even the little companies can buil
a substantial monthly revenue in a relatively shor
amount of time.

When you finally decide which alarm company
you feel the most comfortable with, you're faced with
another choice: whether to lease or buy an alarm system for your home or business. Beware. Don't be
seduced by what might be a low introductory price.
You know that old saying, nothing in life is free? When
acquiring an alarm system, nothing could be more
true. Read your contract carefully. The salespeople pre-
fer to call them "agreements," but as in all written
agreements, they really are binding contracts.
Unfortunately, most of us don't take the time to read
all of the fine print. This is an important document,
and I advise you to read it carefully.

As you're reading through the agreement, you will
stumble upon a clause that describes the time period
for which you are bound. Bound? Yes, very tightly
bound! It can be as long as five years. That's a long
time to be tied into an agreement of any kind. I write
about contracts in depth because you really need to
know how solidly binding they can be. If you decide to
cancel early or simply not pay for the system, there is a
good chance you will end up being sued by the alarm
provider. Before entering into the agreement, ask them
for their policy regarding early cancellation. By the
way, get it in writing.

Let's run the numbers again. I recently saw an
advertisement offering to install an alarm system for
$100 and a monitoring fee of $30 per month. In the fine
print the term of the agreement was listed as 60 months.
So the total that you would really be paying for this
$100 system is really how much? All together now—
$1,900! Not a bad profit.

Please don't get me wrong, I'm as much of a capital-
ist as the next guy. There is nothing wrong with making
a profit as long as the consumer fully understands the
terms and conditions.

So beware of the advertisements that offer you an alarm system at a very low installation price. And know what you are buying. In most cases it is only partial protection, perhaps two or three doors or windows along with a motion detector and, of course, an alarm master control. We know this is not a complete system. So guess what? Surprise! There are add-ons that you can purchase to make it complete. The additional openings and motion detectors really add up. Most of us have seen the low-priced advertisements, perhaps a $100 or $200 installation fee, to lure us into calling for the appointment. Did you know that the national average sale price that is brought in by that type of advertisement is approximately $800? Talking about up-selling!

Another way that the companies profit is by selling your alarm monitoring contract to a bigger alarm company with deep pockets. That way the smaller companies can get cash up front and not have to wait months and months to start showing a profit. This is clarified in the following example:

1) Alarm company "A" charges you $100 to install the alarm system and $20 per month for 60 months.

2) Alarm company "A" then sells your 60-month monitoring contract to alarm company "B" for 30 or 40 times the monthly revenue that you agreed to.

3) Company "A" gets cash up front and no longer has to wait for such a long return on the investment. Company "B" on the other hand is willing to earn the profit of 20 or 30 months worth of revenue by simply having deeper pockets and being able to wait for a longer return on its investment. This arrangement works out well for both companies, but what about you?

As you can see, company "A" is willing to install at a loss initially because it will be able to turn your contract over to company "B" and make a profit as soon as the system is in place. Although this is a good financial

move for struggling or smaller alarm installing com.
nies, it may not be very good for the consumer. Why?
some cases, the transactions are structured in such
way that company "A" will continue to assume the ser
vice obligation. It may not have the motivation to give
you service as readily as it did before it sold you the contract. Sometimes the incentive to go that extra mile
mysteriously melts away.

Another popular way to acquire an alarm system
is to lease rather than purchase. Many people won't
want to pay the added charges associated with leasing and may simply choose to buy because it is generally less expensive in the long run. But leasing has
some advantages. If you lease the system, the alarm
dealer has a greater incentive to provide better service
to you because you are paying a higher monthly rate.
There is customarily a very small installation charge,
and sometimes no installation charge. The alarm
provider may choose to use a leasing company to
carry the lease, or they may carry it themselves. There
is more incentive to provide excellent service when
the dealer is carrying the lease directly because the
downside risk is higher—if you don't get the service
that you were promised, you'll probably take your
business elsewhere. Another advantage to leasing is
the fact that you won't own antiquated equipment 10
years after the installation. It is relatively easy to get
the alarm company to update the equipment as it
becomes available.

I recommend that you buy or lease an alarm system
from a reputable, financially strong company. They will
not need to sell your contract to another organization.
Of course getting a quality installation is also important. Your local alarm association may be helpful in
directing you to one or more of these companies, but I
still think working by referral is always the best way to
go. If a friend or business associate in your community
has had a good experience with a local alarm company,
you should probably check them out.

ou might want to ask the following questions when
mpting to select the right company:

- How long have you been in business? (The longer the better.)

- Do you operate your own alarm monitoring station?

- Does your company have an alarm license? (Many cities and states require some type of licensing.)

- What is the license number? (Are they in good standing?)

- Am I purchasing or leasing this alarm system? When does the title actually transfer to me?

Also, have the salesperson provide you with two references that you can call and talk to about their service and installation practices.

It really is worthwhile for you to go through this drill. You may learn some interesting things.

10 False Alarms

LET'S SAY THAT YOU'RE AT WORK AND YOU GET A PHONE CALL from your monitoring company telling you that the alarm at your home has activated. What should you do? Play Rambo? Reach into your briefcase, pull out your most powerful gun, and head to the ranch for a little burglar hunting? The answer is no! It's always best to wait for the police to arrive and check out the property before entering. One of the most dangerous situations that you can encounter is to confront a burglar

What if you arrive with the police to check out your home. They find no sign of forcible entry, notify you that this is a false alarm, and hand you a ticket with a false alarm fine fee in black and white. False alarm fine? Yes. More and more municipalities are rendering false alarm ordinances with whopping fines.

In one major metropolitan city, it is required that all commercial and residential alarm customers apply for and obtain an alarm permit through the city. The permit is renewable annually at $35. With this particular ordinance in place, if an emergency should occur at your home or business, the monitoring center is required to provide the permit number while dispatching the police. If no permit has been obtained, there will be no ponse by the police department. Three free false alarms per year will be granted, and after that a false alarm fine of $50 per occurrence is charged. Check with your city hall or police department to get permit requirements in your city.

With the possibility of getting hit with such large fines, you will want to take all possible precautions to avoid false alarms. Let's look at what causes them:

- Loose-fitting doors that shake or blow open in the wind.

- Fans or air conditioning that go on after the alarm has been set. They blow on displays and other objects, which the motion detector sees as movement and, depending on its sensitivity, may activate.

- Improper use of the system by the operator. Example: not turning off the system in time upon entering, or taking too long to exit and running out the alarm exit delay period (this is a common problem).

- Poor alarm installation. Example: not soldering wiring connections properly.

- Rodents in the attic eating the insulation off of the wiring. They really love to eat this stuff! (This one is a little offensive, but it *is* a problem.)

When you look at the penalties involved in not having a quality system or service company backing it up, the price is high. So a word of advice: buy your alarm system from a quality organization, and learn to use it properly. My father once told me that if you buy the best, you won't be disappointed. He was right!

11 The Ultimate Circumvention Technique

I GUARANTEE THIS WILL BE ONE OF THE MOST EYE-OPENING chapters in this book. You are about to be introduced to the ultimate circumvention technique.

Alarm systems fall into two categories: *local* and *monitored* systems. Local alarm systems make noise locally at the protected home or business. That is how the name local alarm came about. Brilliant!

By now we all know that a monitored alarm system is one that is monitored at an alarm monitoring facility. It may or may not be operated by the installing alarm company. (Just a quick reminder that both an audible device as well as alarm monitoring is recommended to minimize loss and have an effective system.)

How does the alarm signal get from your home or business to the alarm monitoring station? Through your phone line. The same phone line that you talk on when you call your friends. The same phone line that is usually exposed on the exterior of homes and commercial buildings.

There are two types of phone lines available for the transmission of alarm signals. The most common is the one that we just reviewed. The other is a *leased line*. A leased line is a dedicated telephone line placed between

otected premises and the alarm monitoring sta-
. This involves ordering a usually very costly line
n the phone company that will be used only to mon-
r your security system. Due to the high cost of this
mode of signaling, it is unpopular and rare.

If most alarm systems send signals to the monitoring
station via the same virtually unprotected phone line
that you talk on, most alarm owners are in serious jeop-
ardy of not getting the signal through when they need it
most. Why?

Whether you are at home or work, would you please
do me a big favor? I want you to break and take a walk
outside the building that you are presently in. Go to the
side or rear of the building and observe where the telephone lines enter. Well, do it! This is an important lesson to learn.

The phone lines usually come off a telephone pole
or, if you have underground utilities, up through a piece
of plastic pipe and enter a box that says TELEPHONE on
it. Mystified so far? I thought so. After all, this is very difficult stuff to figure out, especially when the box says
TELEPHONE on it. Please see Figure 35 for assistance.

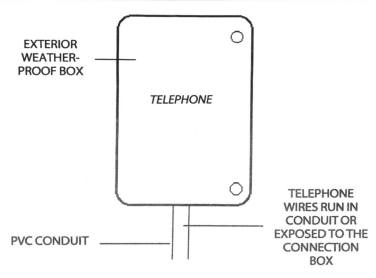

EXTERIOR
WEATHER-
PROOF BOX

TELEPHONE

PVC CONDUIT

TELEPHONE
WIRES RUN IN
CONDUIT OR
EXPOSED TO THE
CONNECTION
BOX

Figure 35. Telephone connection box.

Now that you have found the phone wires, stop a᷉
ask yourself the following questions. If I could find th᷉
phone lines so easily, how fast could the bad guy find
them? If the phone line is so critical in sending the alarm
signal to the monitoring station, shouldn't I be concerned
about its vulnerability? These are valid concerns.

WHAT WOULD HAPPEN IF A BURGLAR FOUND THE
PHONE LINES AND CUT THEM BEFORE HE ENTERED
YOUR HOME OR BUSINESS? Yes, you have just discov-
ered the ultimate circumvention technique.

Burglars are using this trick every day, folks. Lately,
more and more articles and television shows are talking
about telephone line cuts. Burglars have learned where
the lines come into the building and that all they have
to do is cut them. What happens then? Absolutely no
alarm signal will be transmitted to the alarm monitoring station. Nothing! Zilch! Zip! Nada! I thought you
would enjoy that news.

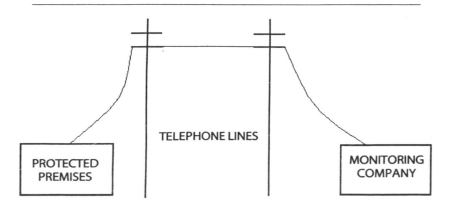

Figure 36. Alarm signal path using conventional phone lines.

Most alarm systems utilize a digital communicator
to transmit the alarm signals to the monitoring station.
The reason that this device is called a digital communicator is because it dials the monitoring station the same
way that you would dial your telephone. This process is
done automatically when the alarm is activated. When

connects with the monitoring station, a code is then sent into the receiving equipment, letting the monitoring operator know what type of problem needs to be addressed. As an example, code number one might represent a fire alarm, code two a burglar alarm, code three a holdup alarm, and so on. If the communications link is cut before the alarm is activated, then naturally these signals cannot get to the alarm monitoring station via the phone line. Make sense?

The alarm industry realizes this is a weak link in the security system. There have been some recent developments to solve the problem, but they are a little late since there are literally millions of digital-dialing alarm systems in use today without any form of protection from phone line circumvention. THIS IS TRULY A MAJOR WEAK LINK!

Fortunately, for a home or business owner, there are some things that can be done to remedy the problem. The alarm system can be installed so that if the phone line is cut, the audible device on the building will activate. But this is only a minor improvement because, as we reviewed earlier, the audible devices are easily taken out.

Another thing that you can do is invest in a dedicated leased line. If the dedicated line is cut, the monitoring center would know that it is your location that is in need of assistance. This option is not recommended, however, due to the fact that it may be cost-prohibitive, depending on how long the phone line needs to go to connect to the monitoring facility. The charges vary depending on the provider, so you may want to check into this with your local telephone company. The other disadvantage is that these lines are becoming a thing of the past. The new fiber optic networks do not allow for this type of use.

One of the more popular new transmission devices to enter the market in recent years is *long-range radio*. It is called long-range radio because it indeed can go a long distance. The range varies by manufacturer, but

generally speaking, if no obstructions such as m
tains or buildings exist, it can go 30 to 40 miles.

Long-range radio is used along with the phone l
to send signals to the monitoring station. If the tel
phone line were cut, the alarm information could go ou
via long-range radio. For you to select this option, the
alarm company or monitoring service you choose
would have to have a long-range radio network in place
(see Figure 37).

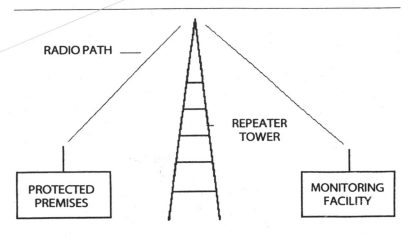

Figure 37. Long-range radio transmission.

There are two types of long-range radio communica-
tion systems: one-way and two-way. One-way radio
transmitters are more prevalent than the two-way
devices. The main reason for this is expense—one-way
devices simply cost less than two-way.

One-way radio does exactly that—it sends signals to
the monitoring station and is not capable of receiving
any type of acknowledgment. The disadvantage of one-
way radio is the uncertainty as to whether the signal is
actually being received at the monitoring facility. You
see, it's like having half of a telephone receiver. If you
only had the speaking half and not the listening half,
you wouldn't be able to communicate both ways.

Two-way radio, on the other hand, is better because

gnal is verifiably received in the monitoring center. signal goes out to the receiving equipment and ds an acknowledgment signal in return, so you know at it has been received successfully. The two-way products cost more and are not as common as one-way, but they are certainly worth the expense. There aren't too many two-way systems in existence because the technology is new, but they are gaining popularity rapidly.

For that extra measure of security, there is one other alternative you can use that is also gaining in popularity and is moderately priced for both the consumer and the alarm-installing company. It is *cellular protection*. The device works just like a cellular phone. If the phone lines are inoperative, it sends a signal to the central monitoring station on the local cellular network. It is very simple to install, and the only charge that you have is the monthly cellular network charge along with any calls that it makes. Of course, there are no telephone lines to circumvent with this cellular backup.

If there is a major lesson to be learned in this chapter, it is to protect your phone line by using one of the above devices. It is a very weak link in your security system and requires special attention. You may have to specifically seek out an alarm dealer that can provide one of these backup devices because not all companies offer radio protection due to the large up-front investment to set up a network. As the threat of phone-line cuts increases, however, so will the need for alternate methods of alarm signal transmission.

12 The Response Nightmare

IN THE PREVIOUS CHAPTER WE LOOKED AT THE MECHANICS OF how the alarm activates and sends signals to the alarm company monitoring center. Now what happens? If the monitoring station receives a burglary signal, the police or private patrol personnel will be dispatched to your location. So begins the response nightmare.

One of the most overlooked areas in this business is not the process of detection but rather the process of responding to the emergency. In major metropolitan cities, I have experienced police response times to alarm calls to take as little as 10 minutes and as long as 5 hours. Take it upon yourself to contact your local police department and ask what the response time is to a burglar alarm call. I think the answer will surprise you.

So you're probably thinking, if the police are supposed to respond with the lights flashing and sirens blaring, what could take them sooooooo long? Sorry to disappoint you again. This only happens on television. No lights and sirens are used in real-life situations. Occasionally I have seen them respond quickly on a holdup or other high-priority call when they have received human verification that the act is in progress.

The reason for this is simple: there are a high

nount of false alarms and very few real alarms. In most major metropolitan cities, the false alarm rate is as high as 90 percent. Why? In some instances it's because the alarm system may need service, but in most cases it is due to operator error. Examples would be turning on the system when it was thought to be off but actually was on. False alarm! Another common one is setting the alarm and proceeding out the door but forgetting something and re-entering to get the item left behind without resetting the system. False alarm! One more. Entering the protected premises with an arm load of items which preclude the operator from turning off the system within the entry delay period. Yet another false alarm! Unfortunately, all of the above contribute to slow response times by the proper authorities.

That is good news for the bad guys and bad news for those trying to get some protection. Unless you live in a small town where the police have excellent funding and absolutely nothing to do, the response to an alarm call may be slow. Thus it is commonly known by burglars that there is really very little chance of their actually getting caught.

Let's look at some of the alternatives:

- You could hire a security guard to live in your home or business 24 hours a day.

- You could build a moat around your property and stock it with burglar-eating alligators.

- You could hire a professional neighborhood armed patrol company to respond to your alarm system.

Of course the latter of the three choices seems to be the most logical way to go, right? Not necessarily. Have you actually seen some of these private patrol guards? It's ugly. Many of them are very poorly paid and have a minimal amount of training. No matter how much you are sold on the fact that patrol response guards are the

---

greatest gift to mankind, they have never had the in
sity or quality training that police officers have he
Police officers go through a lengthy and exhausti
training program to protect your life as well as theirs.

If you decide to hire a patrol service, check them out
carefully. Ask the police department as well as your
alarm provider for referrals. Most states have a licensing
agency that you can call and inquire about any com-
plaints levied against the particular company that you
are considering hiring. You might ask the salesperson
from the patrol company to send his nearest guard to
your house right now, as if the alarm were activating at
this very moment. See what you get. Was the response
timely? Is the response agent armed? Is he in reasonable
physical shape? Does he take a bath every now and
then? Ultimately you need to ask yourself the following
question and feel comfortable with the answer: do I really feel comfortable with this response agent responding
to my home or business with a gun?

Conclusion

Congratulations! You graduate. You now have a good working knowledge of alarm systems and applications. You also now have the powerful knowledge of alarm circumvention. What will you do with this knowledge? Hopefully use it for the purpose for which it was intended—to enable you to design a better security system for you and your family.

After all you have read in this book, I sincerely hope that there is no doubt in your mind that you can definitely benefit by owning an alarm system. Some security is better than none. Now you know what to look for and the questions to ask the prospective alarm provider. Your alarm system design will be well thought out, because you now have the knowledge to make intelligent choices.

Thank you for taking the time to read this book. I hope it adds to the quality of your life.